RELIGIOUS LIVES

Jesus
and
Christianity

Ruth Nason

HODDER
Wayland

an imprint of Hodder Children's Books

Religious Lives

The Buddha and Buddhism   Krishna and Hinduism
Guru Nanak and Sikhism   Moses and Judaism
Jesus and Christianity   Muhammad and Islam

For more information on this series and other Hodder Wayland titles, go to
www.hodderwayland.co.uk

© White-Thomson Publishing Ltd 2006

Produced for Hodder Wayland by White-Thomson Publishing Ltd
Bridgewater Business Centre, 210 High Street, Lewes, East Sussex BN7 2NH, UK

First published in 2006 by Hodder Wayland, an imprint of Hodder Children's Books

This book is adapted from *Jesus and Christianity* (*Great Religious Leaders* series) by Alan Brown,
published by Hodder Wayland in 2002

British Library Cataloguing in Publication Data
Nason, Ruth
Jesus and Christianity, - Adapted Ed. - (Religious Lives)
1. Jesus Christ - Juvenile literature 2. Christianity - Juvenile literature
I.Title II.Brown, Alan, 1944 - 232
ISBN-10: 0750247878
ISBN-13: 9780750247870
Printed in China

Hodder Children's Books
A division of Hodder Headline Limited
338 Euston Road, London NW1 3BH

Title page: Holy week procession in Spain

Picture Acknowledgements: The publisher would like to thank the following for permission to reproduce their pictures:
AKG 4, 6, 7, 8, 9 (Cameraphoto), 10, 11 (Erich Lessing), 12 (S. Domingie), 13 (Cameraphoto), 15, 16, 17 (Cameraphoto), 18 (Erich Lessing), 19 (bottom) (Erich Lessing), 21 (Erich Lessing), 24 (Cameraphoto), 25, 26, 27 (top) (Cameraphoto), 29 (Erich Lessing); Art Directors and Trip Photo Library cover top, 34 (T. Bognar), 40 (H. Rogers), 41 (D. Butcher), 45 (top) P. Treanor, 45 (bottom) D. Butcher; Bridgeman Art Library 14 (Brooklyn Museum of Art), 19 (top) (Brooklyn Museum of Art), 20 (Brooklyn Museum of Art), 22 (Biblioteca Estense, Modena); Britstock-IFA 28 (Gerig), 31 (Braun), 33; Eye Ubiquitous 1 (Brian Harding), 5 (David Cumming), 23 (Bruce Adams), 32 (Adina Tovy Amsel), 35 (bottom) (David Cumming), 36 (David Cumming), 38 (top) (Skjold); Hodder Wayland Picture Library 27 (bottom) (Jim Holmes), 39, 44; Impact Photos 37 (Christophe Bluntzer); James Davis Travel Photography 30, 38 (bottom); Osservatore Romano/Immagionazione/Corbis 35 (top); South American Pictures 43 (Hilary Bradt); Ole Buntzen/ POLFOTO 42.

Graphics and maps by Tim Mayer.

Contents

1   What is Christianity?   4

2   The Life of Jesus   6

3   The Teachings of Jesus   14

4   The Sacred Texts   22

5   The Sacred Places   30

6   Festivals and Celebrations   36

7   Christianity Today   44

Glossary   46

Further Information   47

Index   48

What is Christianity?

The Christian religion began with a man named Jesus. People believed he was the Christ, God in human form.

▲ There is no record of what Jesus looked like. All pictures, like this from the 12th century, are imagined.

Jesus was born in Palestine about 2,000 years ago. The people he lived among were Jewish and their land was part of the Roman Empire.

When Jesus was about 30 years old he began to teach people about God. He told them to make God the ruler of their lives.

The Roman rulers feared trouble, because large crowds gathered to listen to Jesus. Some Jewish religious leaders were worried too, because Jesus spoke as if he was God. Jesus was arrested and put to death on a cross.

◄ Jesus lived in the area that is now Israel and Palestine.

Christians believe that after his death Jesus came alive again. This is called the Resurrection. Finally, he was taken into Heaven.

People who believed in the Resurrection spread the news about it. They wanted to tell other people about Jesus. In this way, Jesus' teachings spread to people who were not Jews and to people in other countries. People who decided to follow his teachings became Christians.

Christ and 'The Way'

When Christians call Jesus 'Christ', it shows that they believe he was the 'Messiah', a leader promised by God, who came to establish God's kingdom on earth.

At first, the Christian religion was called 'The Way', because Jesus taught 'the way' to God. The name Christianity was not used until nearly 100 years after Jesus died.

▼ These Russian Christians are holding religious pictures called icons.

The Life of Jesus

The story of Jesus' life and his teachings are found in the Bible, the Christian holy book.

▲ In this painting Mary and Jesus have a halo, or ring of light, around their head. This is to show that they are holy.

Jesus is born

The angel Gabriel, a messenger from God, told a woman called Mary that she would have a baby son, named Jesus.

At the time, Mary was engaged to Joseph, a carpenter in Nazareth. Mary and Joseph had to go to Bethlehem, to take part in a census. They could not find anywhere to stay, but at last an innkeeper let them sleep in his stable. Jesus was born there.

Angels appeared to some shepherds and told them that Christ had been born. The shepherds went to the stable to see the special baby sent by God.

Some wise men called Magi saw a star and believed it was a sign that a new king had been born. They went to Jerusalem, expecting to find him. They met King Herod, who was worried to hear about a new king. He asked the Magi to tell him when they found the baby, so that he could see him too. In fact, Herod planned to kill him.

The Magi and Joseph had dreams warning them that Herod wanted to kill Jesus. So the Magi did not go back to Herod. Joseph, Mary and Jesus fled to Egypt.

Jesus is presented at the Temple

When Jesus was eight days old, Mary and Joseph took him to the Jewish Temple in Jerusalem. They gave thanks to God for his birth.

In the Temple an old man called Simeon and an old woman called Anna saw the baby Jesus. They said they knew that he was the Christ or Messiah, promised by God.

◀ Joseph takes Mary and Jesus away to Egypt. In the background, Herod's soldiers are killing all children under two, to try to make sure that the new king is killed.

Jesus' childhood

From Egypt, Joseph took Mary and Jesus home to Nazareth. The Bible describes how, at age 12, Jesus went to the Temple in Jerusalem and talked to the religious leaders there. Nothing else is known about his childhood.

Jesus begins to teach

When Jesus was about 30, he was baptized in the River Jordan by his cousin, John the Baptist. A voice from Heaven said, 'This is my own dear Son, with whom I am well pleased'.

Jesus went into the desert for 40 days to think about what God wanted him to do. The Devil tempted him to go against God's will, but Jesus resisted. He was ready to begin his work.

▼ All the time Jesus was in the desert he had nothing to eat. This is called fasting.

This painting shows Jesus calling the fishermen Simon, Andrew and John to be his followers and become 'fishers of people'.

Rejected by his home town

Jesus travelled around the area called Galilee, teaching and healing people. When he went to teach in Nazareth, his home town, people there could not think how he could speak in such a wise way, when he was just the son of Mary and Joseph, the carpenter. Jesus did not perform many healings in Nazareth because the people did not believe in him.

Jesus chose twelve followers or disciples, including Simon (later called Peter) and his brother Andrew, who were fishermen.

Jesus began to teach people. He wanted them to know that God loved and cared for them. He healed people who were sick and even brought people who had died to life again. Acts like these are called miracles.

More and more people heard about Jesus and came to listen to him. Not everyone liked his teaching. It did not always agree with what the Jewish religious leaders said. Some of them became his enemies.

Jesus shares bread and wine with his disciples at the meal called the Last Supper. Judas, who betrayed Jesus, is on the right, with red hair.

The Last Week

After three years Jesus knew that his work was coming to an end. He rode on a donkey into the city of Jerusalem and crowds of people welcomed him, shouting, 'God bless the king who comes in the name of the Lord!'

In the next few days Jesus told his twelve disciples about difficult times to come. At a meal for the Jewish festival of Passover, he said that one of them was going to betray him to his enemies.

At the meal Jesus broke bread and shared wine with the disciples. He told them that, when they ate together in future, they should break bread and drink wine. This would be a way to remember him.

After the meal Jesus and some of the disciples went to the Garden of Gethsemane. Jesus prayed for courage to carry out God's will. Then the disciple called Judas arrived. He had accepted some money for showing the Temple guards where Jesus was. The guards arrested Jesus.

The priests and elders thought that Jesus was a troublemaker and should be killed. They handed him over to Pontius Pilate, the Roman governor.

Pilate examined the evidence against Jesus, then handed him over to his soldiers to be killed. Jesus was crucified – nailed to a wooden cross.

After Jesus' death, his body was taken down, dressed for burial and placed in a tomb. The tomb was closed with a large stone.

▼ Crowds watch Jesus on the cross.

▲ The women find that Jesus' tomb is empty and see an angel there. In many other paintings the tomb is shown as a cave, with the large stone rolled away from its entrance.

The Resurrection

Jesus was crucified on a Friday. On Sunday some women, including Mary, his mother, found that the stone used to close the tomb had been rolled away. They went into the tomb and saw an angel, who said that Jesus had risen.

The women ran to tell the disciples, who did not believe them. Then Peter went into the tomb, saw it was empty and found the cloth that had been wrapped around Jesus' body.

Some time later, two of Jesus' followers were walking along a road. They met a stranger and told him about everything that had happened in Jerusalem. They invited the stranger to join them for a meal and, as he broke the bread, they realized he was Jesus. He disappeared and the two men rushed to Jerusalem to tell the disciples.

Several times Jesus appeared to his disciples. The disciple Thomas said that he could only believe that it was Jesus if he could touch the wounds that Jesus received at his crucifixion. Jesus let him touch the wounds.

Some weeks later Jesus was taken into Heaven. He promised that the Holy Spirit would guide the disciples in the future.

The Trinity

Christians believe that there is only one God, but they refer to God in three ways: (1) as the Father and creator; (2) as the Son, Jesus Christ; and (3) as the Holy Spirit, the power of God in people's lives.

◀ Thomas touches the wound in Jesus' side.

The Teachings of Jesus

Jesus said that people should worship God and try to live in the way that God wants. By doing this, they would belong to the 'Kingdom of God' or the 'Kingdom of Heaven'.

▲ Jesus talks to the crowd on the mountainside.

The Sermon on the Mount

In the Bible, many of Jesus' teachings are found in a section called the Sermon on the Mount. A sermon is a talk about religious matters.

A huge crowd of people gathered to hear Jesus speak. Many hoped that he would heal them of their illnesses. Jesus climbed up the mountain and began to teach.

Jesus said that not only people's actions but also their thoughts are important to God. People should love their enemies, not judge others, and be forgiving. They should always put other people first, caring especially for the poor.

Jesus told stories, called parables, to help people understand his teaching.

Jesus said it was difficult for a rich person to enter the Kingdom of Heaven. The richer someone is, the easier it is for them to think just about themselves.

His strongest words were against hypocrites – people who put on an act of being good or religious – and against people who showed off how 'good' they were.

The Beatitudes

The Beatitudes are part of the Sermon on the Mount in which Jesus talks about the kind of people who are blessed (made happy) by God. For example:

God blesses those people who depend only on him. They belong to the kingdom of heaven!
(Matthew 5: 3)

Parables

Jesus often told stories called parables to help people understand and remember his teaching.

A house on rock and a house on sand

At the end of the Sermon on the Mount Jesus told a parable about one man who built a house on rock and another who built a house on sand. When rain and floods came, the house on rock stood firm but the house on sand collapsed. Jesus said that people who heard his teachings and obeyed them were like the wise man who built his house on rock. People who heard his teachings but did not obey them were like the foolish man who built his house on sand.

▼ In the parable, the Samaritan helps the injured man, takes him to an inn and pays for him to be cared for.

The Good Samaritan

In this parable a Jewish man is beaten up by robbers. Several Jewish people walk by and do not help him. By contrast, a man from Samaria (a Samaritan) does stop to help the man.

Jesus told this story when someone asked: 'I know I

must love my neighbour, but who is my neighbour?'
The story was surprising, for in those days Jewish
people hated the Samaritans.

The Prodigal Son

In this parable the younger of two sons leaves home
with his share of his father's money. He spends it all
and ends up poor and starving. Eventually he decides
to go home, admit he was wrong and ask to be a
worker on his father's farm. However, when his father
sees him coming, he runs out to welcome him and
arranges a feast to celebrate his son's return. Jesus
told this story to show that God will forgive people
completely if they are truly sorry.

▼ In this painting the
father welcomes
home his younger son.
The older son, on the
right, is not happy.

▲ This painting shows the miracle when Jesus brought a man called Lazarus back to life, after he had been dead for four days.

Miracles of healing

In the Bible there are many examples of people being healed by Jesus. People believed that he could heal them.

The friends of a man who could not walk carried the man on his bed to a house where Jesus was teaching. The house was so crowded that they could not get through the door. So they climbed on to the roof, made a hole and lowered the man through it.

Healing the sick

Many people believed that illness was caused by sin or wrongdoing. When Jesus healed people, he told them that their sins were forgiven. Some religious leaders were angry about this. They believed that only God could forgive sins.

► In the time of Jesus, most houses had flat roofs, covered with tiles. The men in the story would have removed some tiles to make a hole in the roof.

Jesus told the man to take up his bed and walk because his sins were forgiven. The man got up and walked home. Everyone who saw this was amazed.

Feeding the 5,000

In this story, Jesus had been teaching a huge crowd of people. He told his disciples to give them something to eat. The disciples said they only had five loaves and two fishes.

Jesus divided the loaves and fishes among more than 5,000 people. Even after everyone had eaten, there was so much food left that it filled twelve baskets.

► In the Bible story, Jesus takes the loaves and fishes and gives thanks to God for them.

Making people think

Jesus wanted to make people think about God and the way they lived. He used vivid images. For example:

It's easier for a camel to go through the eye of a needle than for a rich person to get into God's kingdom.

(Matthew 19: 24)

Some important religious Jews, called Pharisees, thought that Jesus did not follow the Jewish religious rules carefully enough. But Jesus said to them:

Don't suppose that I came to do away with the Law and the Prophets. I did not come to do away with them, but to give them their full meaning.

(Matthew 5: 17)

▼ Jesus argues with a group of Pharisees, who are standing on the right.

Pharisees

Pharisees were Jewish religious teachers who followed Jewish customs and laws very strictly. Some Pharisees were angered by what Jesus said or did, and often they questioned or argued with him. Jesus said some of them were hypocrites: they said one thing but did another.

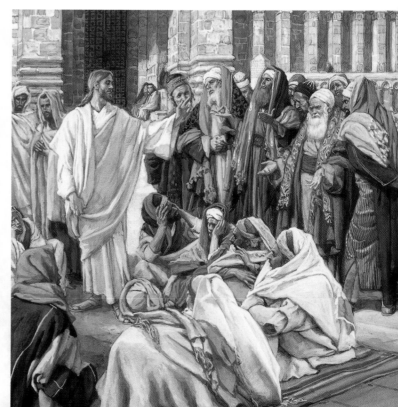

Jesus speaks with the people about the law that said that the woman should be punished by stoning.

Rules and laws

Jesus said that people should think about what God wanted them to do, rather than just following rules and laws. The most important thing was to love God, and then to love each other.

Once Jesus was asked what should happen to a woman who had been unfaithful to her husband. The law said that she should be stoned to death. Jesus said, 'If any of you have never sinned, you throw the first stone at her.' No one answered. Jesus told the woman to go and not do wrong again.

The Sacred Texts

The Christian Bible has two parts, called the Old Testament and the New Testament. Each part is made up of many books, written by many different people over hundreds of years.

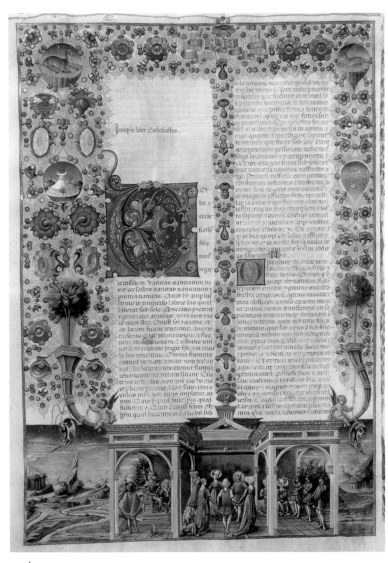

▲ This page is from an Italian Bible, handwritten in the fifteenth century.

The Old Testament

The Old Testament is nearly the same as the Jewish Bible. It begins with the book called Genesis, which starts with the story of God creating the world. Other books are about Moses and other prophets who spoke to people about God.

The New Testament

The first books in the New Testament are about the life and teachings of Jesus. The later books show how people should follow his teachings.

Reading the Bible

The Old Testament was first written in Hebrew. The New Testament was first written in Greek, about 100 years after the

▲ A Bible passage is read out in most church services.

life of Jesus. But the Bible has been translated into every known language so that all Christians can read it.

Some Christians believe that everything in the Bible is factually true. Others believe that the writers used stories and symbols to tell of God's love for the world.

An influential book

Some phrases that we use in English today came from a version of the Bible called the King James Bible, published in 1611 CE.

The Gospels

The first four books of the New Testament are called the Gospels. 'Gospel' means 'good news' and Christians say that these books were written to tell the 'good news' about Jesus' life and resurrection.

The Gospels were written between 30 and 100 years after Jesus' death, by four followers of his teaching: Matthew, Mark, Luke and John. Each tells the same basic story of Jesus' life, death and resurrection, but emphasizes different things.

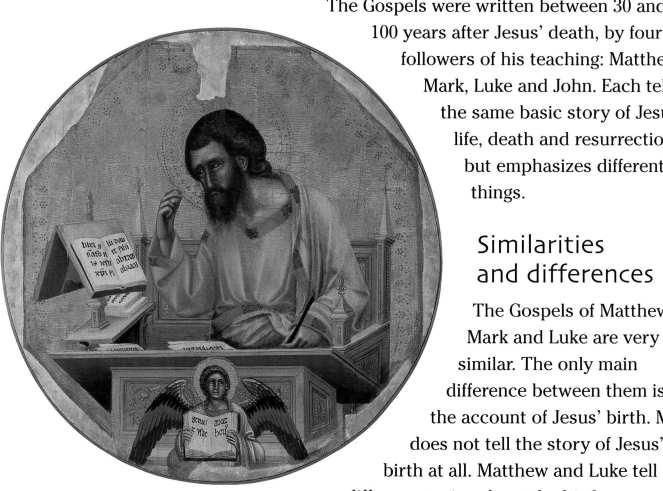

▲ This fourteenth-century painting represents Matthew writing his Gospel.

Similarities and differences

The Gospels of Matthew, Mark and Luke are very similar. The only main difference between them is in the account of Jesus' birth. Mark does not tell the story of Jesus' birth at all. Matthew and Luke tell different stories about the birth.

John's Gospel contains stories and teachings that are not in the other three Gospels. There are no parables in John's Gospel and the order of events is different. Jesus makes long speeches about himself and most of the miracles are different too.

Emphasizing different things

Mark's Gospel gives the impression that Jesus wanted to spread God's message quickly.

According to Matthew's Gospel, Jesus commanded his followers to go out and teach God's message to all nations, not just the Jews.

Luke's Gospel tells how Jesus cared for the poor and people who suffer. It also gives more attention to the women who played a part in Jesus' life.

▼ This Russian painting of John with his symbol, the eagle, was painted in the nineteenth century.

Symbols of the Gospel writers

In paintings of the Gospel writers, symbols are often used to identify them. Matthew's symbol is a human face. Mark's symbol is a roaring lion. Luke's symbol is an ox. John's symbol is an eagle.

Paul's letters

Many of the books in the New Testament are letters sent by a Christian called Paul.

Before he became a Christian, Paul was called Saul. He was a Pharisee (see page 20). He hated what Jesus taught and he persecuted Christians. But one day Saul had a vision of Jesus speaking to him. He became an apostle, someone who goes out to spread Jesus' message. Saul changed his name to Paul.

Paul travelled far and wide around the Mediterranean. His letters are to Christians who began to gather together in places such as Rome and Corinth. There are also letters to people called Timothy, Titus and Philemon. It is thought that Paul died in Rome in 60–65 CE.

▲ In this painting Paul is represented with a halo (see page 6).

▲ This painting represents the apostles Paul (left) and Peter. Peter was one of Jesus' first disciples.

Explaining Jesus' life

Paul's letters explain his beliefs about Jesus, the Son of God. Paul said that Jesus' life and death showed how powerfully God loves all people. Jesus mended the relationship between God and people, which had been broken by people's sin.

Faith, hope and love

Paul wrote that Christians must have faith, hope and love. The most important of these is love. Paul used many words to describe this love: for example, patient, kind, unselfish, forgiving, never ending.

▲ Belief in Jesus is the most important part of Christianity.

The Lord's Prayer

Jesus gave his disciples a simple prayer to say, calling God 'Father'. This prayer, known as 'The Lord's Prayer' or 'Our Father', is still used by Christians everywhere:

Our Father in heaven, help us to honour your name.
Come and set up your kingdom,
So that everyone on earth will obey you, as you are obeyed in heaven.
Give us our food for today.
Forgive us for doing wrong, as we forgive others.
Keep us from being tempted and protect us from evil.

(Matthew 6: 9–13)

▼ At this church service the people are standing to say some prayers. Christians also kneel to pray. They may put their hands together and bow their heads.

God's love

This verse from John's Gospel sums up what Christians believe:

God loved the people of this world so much that he gave his only Son, so that everyone who has faith in him will have eternal life.

(John 3: 16)

Love your neighbours

Jesus was a Jew and followed the commandments in the Jewish Bible (see page 22). He said that the two most important commandments are:

Love the Lord your God with all your heart, soul, strength and mind ...
Love your neighbours as much as you love yourself.

(Mark 12: 29-31)

Christians also follow these commandments, from the Old Testament of the Christian Bible.

Favourite passages

Many Christians have favourite Bible passages. They may be passages that they read for comfort, to give thanks, or just to feel that they are close to Jesus.

▼ Stained-glass windows in churches often show pictures of Bible stories. This one shows the birth of Jesus (bottom) and the Magi's visit (top).

The Sacred Places

The city of Jerusalem is sacred for Jews, Christians and Muslims. For Christians it is sacred because Jesus was crucified and rose from the dead there.

Jesus and Jerusalem

One estimate is that 30,000 people lived in Jerusalem at the time of Jesus. At festival times this may have risen to 120,000.

◀ Parts of Jerusalem have hardly changed since the time of Jesus.

Jews in Jerusalem

Jerusalem is where King Solomon built the first Jewish Temple. It was destroyed, but a new one was built, which was there in the time of Jesus.

In 70 CE the Romans destroyed the second Temple. Only its western wall still stands. This is a holy place for Jews and many go to pray there.

Jesus went to Jerusalem as a boy (see page 8). At the end of his teaching, he went there for the festival of Passover. He rode into the city on a donkey (see page 10).

In those days, Jews went to the Temple to give thanks to God by making sacrifices of birds, sheep and goats. Jesus found money-changers and traders at the Temple, selling these animals. He was angry and said they were turning God's house into a place of robbers.

▼ Some people believe that the Church of the Holy Sepulchre in Jerusalem is built on the spot where Jesus was buried.

Jesus was crucified in Jerusalem at a place called Golgotha.

Christian pilgrims

Many Christians visit Jerusalem, especially at Easter (see page 36). They walk the route that Jesus walked to Golgotha. It is called the *Via Dolorosa*, which means the Road of Sorrows.

They also visit the Church of the Holy Sepulchre.

Galilee

Jesus lived in the area called Galilee, in the north of present-day Israel (see map, page 4). The Gospels say that Jesus taught in the open air and in the synagogue at Capernaum. There is no account of him going to the main towns of Tiberias and Sepphoris. He may have avoided them because the king there, called Herod, had executed John the Baptist.

▼ Today farms and buildings cover the area by the Sea of Galilee.

► Fishermen work on the Sea of Galilee today, like some of Jesus' disciples 2,000 years ago.

In the time of Jesus, Jews and non-Jews lived in Galilee. There was conflict between Jews and the people of Samaria, to the south of Galilee. This made Jews nervous of travelling through Samaria on their way to Jerusalem.

The Sea of Galilee is actually a lake, also called Lake Tiberias or Lake Gennesaret. Three of Jesus' disciples came from Bethsaida, a village by the lake. The village name means 'House of Fishing'.

Pilgrims in Galilee

Christians who visit Galilee are able to imagine what it was like 2,000 years ago, when crowds of people gathered on the hills to listen to Jesus' teaching.

'Galilee of the Nations'

Camel trains carried goods for trade across Galilee and so people from many lands visited and settled there. In the Bible, Galilee is called 'Galilee of the Nations' because of its mixture of people. Galileans were thought to be troublesome. The Pharisees thought that they didn't follow the Jewish law very carefully.

Rome

Rome was the centre of the Mediterranean area and of Europe at the time of Jesus.

It is likely that Jesus' disciple and apostle Peter went to Rome and was killed there. The apostle Paul (see page 26) was taken to Rome for trial and he was probably executed there too.

The Romans persecuted Christians, like Peter and Paul, for 250 years. To avoid this, Christians in Rome worshipped secretly in underground burial places called catacombs. However, in the early 4th century CE, the Roman Emperor Constantine became a Christian. After that, Rome became the most important city in the Christian world.

▲ Christian pilgrims from all over the world visit St Peter's Church in Rome.

Vatican City

Today Rome is still special for Christians who are Roman Catholics. The leader of the Roman Catholic Church, the Pope, lives in Vatican City, a state within the city of Rome.

The Pope takes the title 'Bishop of Rome', which was first given to the apostle Peter.

▲ The Pope blesses a crowd at St Peter's Church.

▼ The leader of the Russian Orthodox Church is called the Patriarch.

Different churches

Christianity became the official religion of the Roman Empire in the late fourth century, but differences developed. Churches in the east believed that they kept to the true or 'orthodox' way. They did not accept changes that church leaders in Rome wanted to make. In 1054 CE the eastern and western churches split into the Orthodox Churches and the Roman Catholic Church.

In the sixteenth century there was another split. Some churches broke away from the Roman Catholic Church to become Protestant.

Festivals and Celebrations

The main festival is Easter, when Christians remember the death and resurrection of Jesus.

Christians in India take part in a procession on Good Friday.

Preparing for Easter

Christians prepare for Easter during a 40-day period called Lent. Many do extra Bible study. Forty days is the time that Jesus spent in the desert before he started to teach (see page 8). He resisted the Devil's temptations and some Christians remember this by giving up something that they really like for the whole of Lent.

Holy week

The week before Easter is called Holy Week. Christians remember the last week of Jesus' life and re-enact some of the events to try to share his suffering.

On Palm Sunday they think about Jesus riding into Jerusalem on a donkey (see page 10). The crowds welcomed him like a king and threw palm branches in his path. At many church services on Palm Sunday, people are given crosses made of palm leaves.

The Thursday of Holy Week is called Maundy Thursday. Jesus washed the feet of his disciples on this day and that is often re-enacted at church services.

Then, on Good Friday, Christians remember how Jesus was crucified. There are solemn processions, carrying a cross.

Easter Day

Easter Day is the Sunday after Good Friday. Around the world people take part in joyful church services to celebrate that 'Jesus is risen'. Christians believe that Jesus rose from the dead and is alive today.

▼ These Greek women are using flowers to celebrate Easter Day.

In some churches, Christians light special Advent candles on the four Sundays of Advent.

Christmas

Christmas is when Christians celebrate the birth of Jesus. In the west Christmas Day is December 25, but the actual date of Jesus' birth is not known. Emperor Constantine (see page 34) decided to celebrate it at the same time as the Roman winter festival of the Unconquered Sun.

Before Christmas Day there are four weeks called Advent. Like Lent before Easter, Advent is a serious time when Christians think about their lives and what they want to put right.

Late on Christmas Eve and on Christmas Day morning there are joyful church services to welcome Jesus and thank God for his birth.

Epiphany

At Epiphany, on January 6, Christians remember the story of the Magi, who went to visit and worship Jesus (see pages 6-7).

At Christmas some churches make a Nativity scene with figures of people from the story of Jesus' birth.

Saint Nicholas

Saint Nicholas lived in the 4th century. There is a story that he wanted to give a gift to show his love for Jesus. God told him to give something secretly to poor children instead. The story of St Nicholas, also known as Santa Claus, became linked with Christmas.

▲ In this Christmas parade a man is dressed as Saint Nicholas.

Candlemas

At Candlemas, on February 2, Christians remember how Mary and Joseph took the baby Jesus to the Temple and met Simeon and Anna (see page 7).

Festival dates

Dates of Christian festivals vary around the world. For example, some Christians celebrate Christmas twelve days later than December 25. Most Orthodox Churches celebrate Christmas on January 7.

Pentecost

Christians celebrate Pentecost on the seventh Sunday after Easter. They remember the story of how God sent the Holy Spirit (see page 13) to Jesus' disciples.

This happened after Jesus had died and gone to Heaven. Now the disciples needed courage and strength to go out and become apostles, teaching other people about Jesus. One day they were all together in Jerusalem when:

Suddenly there was a noise from heaven like the sound of a mighty wind! It filled the house where they were meeting. Then they saw what looked liked fiery tongues moving in all directions ...

(Acts of the Apostles 2: 2–3)

The 'fiery tongues' or flames came to rest on each of the disciples. The disciples were filled with the Holy Spirit and began to talk in many languages. People from many countries were

◀ This church has been decorated for Pentecost with banners showing pictures of flames.

staying in Jerusalem and came to listen. They could all understand the disciples' words.

Pentecost is often seen as the birthday of the Christian Church. Another name for it, in the UK, is Whitsun (from 'White Sunday'). It was a tradition for new Christians to join the Church on that day and they wore white clothes for the ceremony.

The Pentecostal Movement

The Pentecostal movement is a Christian group which began in the USA over 100 years ago. Its members believe in the power of the Holy Spirit to heal people and make people 'speak in tongues' today.

▼ Worshippers sing and pray at a Pentecostal church in Tanzania.

Many Christian churches have ceremonies to mark stages in a person's life.

Baptism and confirmation

Jesus was baptized in the River Jordan (see page 8) and baptism has always been used to mark the fact that someone has become a Christian. In some baptisms, water is sprinkled on the person. In others, the person is dipped under the water.

In many churches, babies are baptized. This shows that the baby has become part of the Christian Church. The baby's parents and godparents promise to bring up the child to be a Christian.

In other churches only adults are baptized. The person makes their own promises to live as a Christian. This is called 'Believer's baptism'.

▲ A priest baptizes a baby in a church in Denmark.

Some churches have a confirmation ceremony for teenagers or adults to confirm the promises made for them at their baptism.

▲ After their marriage ceremony in a church, this couple in Peru walk on sacred land at the side of the church.

Marriage

At a Christian marriage ceremony the couple make promises to each other before God.

Funerals

When someone dies there is a funeral to say thank you to God for that person's life and to offer their soul up to God. Funerals are sad occasions for people who have lost a loved one. At the same time there can be joy because Christians believe that the dead person has 'gone to live with God'.

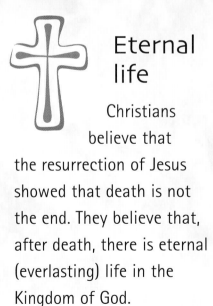

Eternal life

Christians believe that the resurrection of Jesus showed that death is not the end. They believe that, after death, there is eternal (everlasting) life in the Kingdom of God.

Christianity Today

Christianity has spread all around the world. It is the main religion in the West and in the Americas. Recently there has been a rapid increase in the numbers of Christians in Africa and China. The religion is less strong in India and the Far East. Only 2 per cent of people in India are Christians.

▲ Christians take part in a religious procession in Spain.

Church-going

In Europe, fewer people are going to church than in the past. In the UK, only about 8 per cent of people attend church, although 42 million (70 per cent) claim to be Christian. Church-going is still popular in the USA and Central and South America. In parts of the USA 45–50 per cent of people go to church.

Working together

Over time Christians split into different Churches, each claiming to understand Jesus better than the others. However, in the 20th century, the Churches realized that they should work together more. In 1949 the World Council of Churches was formed. This type of working together is called 'ecumenical' (meaning 'one world'). Churches may continue to have different views but they try to work as 'one body'. They all have the same aim: to teach the 'good news' about Jesus.

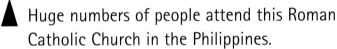

▲ Huge numbers of people attend this Roman Catholic Church in the Philippines.

▼ A simple building serves as a church in Tanzania.

Facts and figures

There are over two billion Christians in the world. Half are Roman Catholic and about 500 million of these live in Central and South America. Most Christians today are non-white and live in the Southern Hemisphere. There are over 22,000 different Christian groups or sects.

Glossary

angel a heavenly being, believed to be sent by God to do or say something.

apostle a person sent out to teach the Christian message.

baptize to perform a ceremony using water as a symbol of a new start. The person may be dipped under water or water is sprinkled on them. John the Baptist baptized people as a sign that they were making a new start in following God. Since Jesus' death and resurrection, people have been baptized as a sign that they are starting a new life as a Christian.

betray to secretly go against a person who trusts you, for example by giving information about the person to an enemy.

CE in the Common Era, used in dates in place of AD ('Anno Domini', Latin for 'in the year of our Lord' (Jesus). Using CE recognizes that many people follow religions other than Christianity.

census an official count of people in a country.

church a group of Christians who worship together; or a building used for Christian worship. With capital letters, the Christian Church means all Christians worldwide.

crucified put to death by being nailed or bound to a cross.

Devil the supreme spirit of evil.

disciple someone who followed Jesus during his life. Jesus chose 12 disciples to help him in his teaching. Later they became apostles.

Heaven the place of peace where God rules and people live together with God. Also called 'the Kingdom of Heaven' or 'the Kingdom of God'.

holy concerned with God or religion, sacred.

icon a painting of Jesus, Mary or a saint, used in worship, especially in Orthodox Churches.

miracles extraordinary and welcome events, impossible to explain by laws of nature or science.

Nativity the birth of Jesus, or a picture of the scene in the stable, with Mary, Joseph, shepherds, Magi and angels.

Orthodox Churches one main branch of the Christian Church, including the Russian Orthodox, Greek Orthodox and other churches.

parable a story about something ordinary and everyday, used to explain a more difficult idea.

persecute to attack, kill, or make life difficult for someone, because of dislike for the religion or group that they belong to.

pilgrims people who travel to a holy place for religious reasons.

prophets people who speak for God and tell people what God wants.

Protestant Churches one main branch of the Christian Church, including Anglican, Baptist, Methodist and other churches.

resurrection rising from the dead.

Roman Catholic Church one main branch of the Christian Church, led by the Pope, in Rome.

sin going against God's wishes.

soul the spiritual part of a person.

synagogue a building where Jewish people meet, pray and study.

Further Information

Books

2000 Years. The Christian Faith in Britain by Nicola Currie (Lion Publishing, 1999)

21st Century Religions: Christianity by David Self (Hodder Wayland, 2005)

Celebrate! Easter by Mike Hirst (Hodder Wayland, 2002)

Holy Cities: Jerusalem by Nicola Barber (Alpha Books/Evans Publishing, 2003)

Holy Cities: Rome by Nicola Barber (Alpha Books/Evans Publishing, 2003)

Sacred Texts: The Bible and Christianity by Alan Brown (Evans Publishing Group, 2003)

Storyteller: Christian Stories by Anita Ganeri (Evans Publishing Group, 2000)

The Facts About Christianity by Alison Cooper (Hodder Children's, 2004)

The Jesus Encyclopedia by Lois Rock (Lion Publishing, 2005)

World of Festivals: Christmas by Catherine Chambers (Evans Publishing Group, 2004)

World of Festivals: Easter by Catherine Chambers (Evans Publishing Group, 2004)

Resources for teachers

http://www.reonline.org.uk
A 'family of websites' including some for teachers and some for pupils. Serves as a gateway to over 300 RE resources drawn from all over the web.

http://www.culham.ac.uk
Website of Culham Institute which promotes good practice in, and awareness of, RE.

http://www.natsoc.org.uk
Website of National Society (Church of England) for Promoting RE.

http://re-xs.ucsm.ac.uk
RE Exchange Service (linked to National Grid for Learning) with a 'Teachers' Cupboard' resource page.

http://www.stapleford-centre.org
An independent education centre, focusing on training for teachers.

http://www.theredirectory.org.uk

BBC Education produces schools media resources on different faiths. See:
http://www.bbc.co.uk/schools

Channel 4 produces schools media resources on different faiths, including *Animated World Faiths*. Download catalogue from:
http://www.channel4.com/learning

Index

Advent 38
angels 6, 12
Anna 7, 39
apostles 26, 27, 34, 35, 40

baptism 42
  of Jesus 8, 42
Beatitudes 15
Bethlehem 4, 6
Bethsaida 4, 33
Bible 6, 8, 14, 18, 19, 22, 23, 29,
  33, 36
    New Testament 22, 24, 25, 26
    Old Testament 22, 29
birth of Jesus 6, 7, 24, 29, 38
bread and wine 10

Candlemas 39
Capernaum 4, 32
Christ 4, 5, 6, 7
Christmas 38, 39
Church of the Holy Sepulchre 31
confirmation 42
Constantine, Emperor 34, 38
cross 4, 11, 36, 37
crucifixion 13, 31, 37

death 43
desert 8, 36
Devil 8, 36
disciples 9, 10, 11, 12, 13, 19, 27,
  33, 34, 37, 40

Easter 31, 36, 37, 40
Epiphany 38
eternal life 29, 43

feeding the 5,000 19
fishermen 9, 33
funerals 43

Galilee 4, 9, 32, 33
Good Friday 37
Gospels 24, 25, 32

healing 9, 18-19, 41
Heaven 5, 8, 13, 40
Herod 7
Holy Spirit 13, 40, 41
Holy Week 36, 37

Jerusalem 4, 7, 10, 12, 30, 31,
  33, 36, 40, 41
Jewish religious leaders 4, 8, 9,
  18, 20 (see also Pharisees)
John the Baptist 8, 32
Joseph 6, 7, 8, 9, 39
Judas 10, 11

Kingdom of God/Heaven 14, 15,
  43

Last Supper 10
Lent 36
Lord's Prayer 28
love 14, 17, 21, 23, 27, 29, 39

Magi 6, 7, 29, 38
marriage 43
Mary 6, 7, 8, 9, 12, 39
Maundy Thursday 37
Messiah 5, 7
miracles 9, 18, 25

Nazareth 4, 6, 8, 9
Nicholas, Saint 39

Orthodox Churches 35, 39

Palm Sunday 36
parables 15, 16, 17, 24
Paul 26, 27, 34
Pentecost 40, 41
Peter 9, 12, 27, 34, 35
Pharisees 20, 36, 33
poor 14, 25, 39
Pope 35
Protestant Churches 35

Resurrection 5, 12, 36, 43
Roman Catholics 35, 45
Rome 34, 35

Samaria/Samaritans 4, 16, 33
Sermon on the Mount 14, 16
Simeon 7, 39
sin 18, 19, 27

Temple, Jerusalem 7, 8, 30, 31,
  39
temptations 8, 36
Thomas 13
tomb of Jesus 11, 12, 37
Trinity 13

Vatican City 35
Via Dolorosa 31

World Council of Churches 45